AVOIDING DEATH TAXES
AND
INCOME TAXES, TOO

The 2017 Tax Act and the New Strategies It Provides

Raymond E. Saunders

Joseph A. Zarlengo

David L. Reich

Ted A. Koester

Shannon L. Hartzler

David W. Trailov

Timothy J. Edmier

Attorneys

Lawrence Kamin, LLC

Lawrence Kamin is a mid-sized, Chicago-based law firm. We tailor sophisticated, cost-effective legal advice and tax and estate planning strategies to meet the goals of wealthy individuals, families and business owners. Planning for the accumulation, conservation and ultimate distribution of wealth is a focus area of Lawrence Kamin.

For more information about our practice areas and attorneys, please visit our website: **www.LawrenceKaminLaw.com**.

AVOIDING DEATH TAXES *AND INCOME TAXES, TOO*

TABLE OF CONTENTS

THE AUTHORS

Raymond E. Saunders
Partner

Phone: 312-924-4243
Email: resaunders@lawrencekaminlaw.com
Office: 300 S. Wacker Drive, Suite 500
Chicago, IL 60606

Focus Areas: Income Tax, Estate & Gift Tax, Mergers & Acquisitions

Overview

For more than 50 years, clients have counted Raymond E. Saunders among their most trusted advisors, not just in law, but in all aspects of their business.

Ray centers his practice around corporate structure, business transactions, mergers and acquisitions, income tax, trusts, estate and gift tax (including cross-generational transfer and ownership of business). While Ray is technically proficient as a Certified Public Accountant, his strength lies in is his pragmatic approach and ability to craft effective strategies to address complex problems.

Education

Northwestern University School of Law, J.D., *cum laude*, 1956
    Order of the Coif, Editor, Northwestern University Law Review
Northwestern University, B.S., Accounting, *cum laude*, 1953

Honors

Illinois Silver Medal, 1954 CPA Examination (2nd highest score in Illinois)
Elijah Watt Sells Award, 1954 CPA Examination (top 10 score in the U.S.)

Bar Admissions

State of Illinois

Professional Memberships & Affiliations

Adjunct Professor, Northwestern University School of Law
    Structuring Transactions – Purchase and Sale of a Business
Chicago Bar Association

Joseph A. Zarlengo
Partner

Phone: 312-924-4247
Email: jzarlengo@lawrencekaminlaw.com
Office: 300 S. Wacker Drive, Suite 500
              Chicago, IL 60606

Focus Areas: Business & Corporate Services, Estate Planning, Tax Controversies

Overview

More than 30 years of legal and tax experience combined with an amiable personality has made Joseph A. Zarlengo an outstanding consigliere in reconciling contrasting business differences and opposing views in stressful family situations. Joe advises business clients on tax and business matters, as well as entity formation and ownership structure, asset protection and tax savings. He also assists clients with wealth preservation strategies and business succession planning, as well as the formation of family foundations and other philanthropic entities to meet charitable objectives.

Education

New York University School of Law, L.L.M. Taxation, 1986
The John Marshall Law School, J.D., 1985
California State University, B.A., 1982

Honors

The John Marshall Law School, J.D., 1985, High Distinction; Law Review Honors; National Moot Court Competitor; Mugel Tax Competition – 4th best brief, 1985

Bar Admissions & Court Admissions

State of Illinois; United States Tax Court

Professional Memberships & Affiliations

American Bar Association; Illinois State Bar Association; Chicago Bar Association South Suburban Estate Planning Council, 1992-present

Community Service

Chicago Volunteer Legal Services, Member; Knights of Columbus Council, No. 9770, Co-chair; Fund Raising for Special Needs Citizens; Treatment Alternatives for Safe Communities (TASC), Donor Cultivation

David L. Reich
Partner

Phone: 312-924-4246
Email: dreich@lawrencekaminlaw.com
Office: 300 S. Wacker Drive, Suite 500
         Chicago, IL 60606

Focus Areas: Business & Corporate Services, Estate
Planning, Real Estate

Overview
David L. Reich has represented countless clients in transactional matters,
including commercial and industrial real estate transactions, commercial,
office, retail and industrial leasing, and real estate lending on behalf of lenders
and borrowers. David maintains a focused practice in estate and gift-tax
planning and estate and trust administration, business succession planning and
general corporate and business transactions and contracts.

Education
Northwestern University School of Law, J.D., 1991
Indiana University, B.S., Finance, 1985

Bar Admissions & Court Admissions
State of Illinois; United States District Court – Northern District of Illinois

Professional Memberships & Affiliations
Adjunct Professor, Northwestern University School of Law
    Structuring Transactions – Purchase and Sale of a Business
Chicago Bar Association

Community Service
Israel Cancer Research Fund, Board of Directors; Modestus Bauer Foundation,
Board of Directors; Highland Park Community Foundation, Board of Directors

THE AUTHORS

Ted A. Koester
Partner

Phone: 312-924-4257
Email: tkoester@lawrencekaminlaw.com
Office: 300 S. Wacker Drive, Suite 500
          Chicago, IL 60606

Focus Areas: Business & Corporate Services, Estate Planning, Trust & Estate Administration, Probate

Overview
Ted A. Koester takes a pragmatic and preventative approach to developing comprehensive and cost-efficient solutions for clients. He primarily focuses on estate and asset preservation, helping individuals and business owners devise strategic plans to protect their wealth and assets, plan for the future of their businesses, and avoid unnecessary taxes, administration and legal fees. Ted often provides legal representation for clients embroiled in estate and trust administration matters. He has experience representing both fiduciaries and beneficiaries through numerous probate and non-probate proceedings.

Education
Seton Hall University, School of Law, J.D., 1998
Eastern Illinois University, B.S., Financial Management, 1994

Bar Admissions & Court Admissions
State of Illinois; State of Wisconsin

Professional Memberships & Affiliations
American Bar Association
Illinois State Bar Association, Trusts & Estates Section, Business Advice and
    Financial Planning Section
Chicago Bar Association, Trust Law Committee Member,
    Probate Committee Member, Speaker
Chicago Estate Planning Council, Board Member 2013-present
Seton Hall Alumni Association, Chicago Chapter,
    President & Board Member
National Business Institute, Speaker

Shannon H. Hartzler
Partner

Phone: 312-924-4254
Email: shartzler@lawrencekaminlaw.com
Office: 300 S. Wacker Drive, Suite 500
Chicago, IL 60606

Focus Areas: Estate Planning, Trust & Estate
Administration

Overview
Shannon H. Hartzler concentrates her practice on estate planning and trust and estate administration. She has advised clients on a wide array of trust restructuring, business succession planning, asset protection and philanthropic issues. In addition, Shannon has significant experience advising individuals and financial institutions on estate and trust administration matters. She guides trustees, executors and beneficiaries through the complexities of administration and assists her clients with the probate process, asset transfers and the preparation of estate tax returns.

Education
Valparaiso University Law School, J.D., *summa cum laude*, 2007
The Boston Conservatory, Masters of Music in Musical Theater, 1999
Goshen College, B.A., 1997

Bar Admissions
State of Illinois

Professional Memberships & Affiliations
American Bar Association, Trust & Estates Section
Illinois State Bar Association
Chicago Bar Association
Chicago Estate Planning Council

Community Service
Legacy Partners, supporting Lurie Children's Hospital, Member

THE AUTHORS

David W. Trailov
Associate

Phone: 312-924-4264
Email: dtrailov@lawrencekaminlaw.com
Office: 300 S. Wacker Drive, Suite 500
Chicago, IL 60606

Focus Areas: Estate Planning, Trust Administration, Probate, Guardianship, State and Local Tax

Overview

David W. Trailov advises clients on how best to pass assets to future generations while implementing strategies and best practices to minimize estate and income taxes, and protect clients' assets from potential creditors. David also represents guardians in both adult and minor guardianships. With past experience as a Fiduciary Officer at a large banking institution, David offers clients a unique perspective on trust and estate administration. He also advises clients on state and local tax matters, including sales/use tax, franchise tax, and income tax.

Education

Chicago Kent College of Law, L.L.M. Taxation, with honors, 2012
Golden Gate University, School of Law, J.D., 2005
Indiana University, B.S., 2002

Bar Admissions & Court Admissions

State of Illinois; State of California; United States District Court – Northern District of Illinois

Professional Memberships & Affiliations

Illinois State Bar Association
Chicago Bar Association

Timothy J. Edmier
Of Counsel

Phone: 312-924-4259
Email: tedmier@lawrencekaminlaw.com
Office: 300 S. Wacker Drive, Suite 500
Chicago, IL 60606

Focus Areas: Business & Corporate Services,
Tax Controversies, Estate Planning

Overview

Timothy J. Edmier is a corporate and tax attorney who focuses his practice in estate planning, asset protection, federal and state taxation and construction law. He advises corporate and business clients on asset protection, entity structure and formation, as well as administrative tax controversy matters. Tim has represented both individuals and businesses on various audit matters, and advises many clients with respect to mechanic's liens on both private and public projects.

Education

Northwestern University School of Law, L.L.M., Taxation, 2007
Chicago Kent College, J.D., 2001
University of Illinois, B.S., Finance, 1996

Bar Admissions & Court Admissions

State of Illinois; United States Supreme Court

Professional Memberships & Affiliations

Illinois State Bar Association
Chicago Bar Association
North Suburban Bar Association

AVOIDING DEATH TAXES
AND
INCOME TAXES, TOO

The 2017 Tax Act and
the New Strategies It Provides

Acknowledgements

Inez Saunders, the wife of Ray Saunders, provided the inspiration and motivation for both this book and the 2014 book *Avoiding Death Taxes*. For *Avoiding Death Taxes,* Inez contributed the very apt subtitle, "You Can't Take It With You". She suggested that the present book answer a much more important concern: "Give me more funds to spend during my lifetime" by reducing income taxes. The Tax Cuts and Jobs Act enacted in December 2017 answered her wish.

We thank those that provided special assistance. Promila Israni, a long-time legal assistant at Lawrence Kamin, enthusiastically typed and retyped the many drafts. Kathy Koester, our very capable Marketing Director, did a wonderful job with art direction and handled a multitude of details to help finalize this publication. Also, Anna Strelka, who is a splendid author of fiction, provided valuable editorial assistance, as always. We are grateful for their efforts.

Introduction

In the conclusion to our 2014 book Avoiding Death Taxes, we compared the struggle between wealthy individuals and U.S. governments over the disposition of their wealth to the famous battle between David and Goliath.[1] In December 2017, Congress passed and President Trump signed the Tax Cuts and Jobs Act (the "Tax Act"), thereby changing many rules. By passing the Tax Act, Goliath introduced new weapons and strategies into David's already extensive arsenal. In this book we will review this expanded arsenal, arming the taxpayer to defeat the government's quest for income and estate taxes.

---

[1] Some scholars believe the story of David and Goliath was written in the sixth century BC, but that it actually took place much earlier. According to Hebrew scholars, the most popular legends about David, including his killing of Goliath, his affair with Bathsheba, and his ruling of a United Monarchy of Israel rather than just Judah, are the creation of those who lived generations after him. Archaeologists have established that Gath, traditional home of Goliath, was destroyed in the ninth century BC, which means the story is set in the ninth century or earlier. David appears to be quite a young man, probably in his teens, when he slew Goliath. Since David's birth is conventionally placed around 1040 BC, the battle of David and Goliath probably took place around 1020 BC.

Chapter 1

Increase in the Estate Tax, Gift Tax and
Generation Skipping Tax Exemption

For transfers made and decedents who pass after 2017, the exemption has doubled from approximately $5.6 million to $11.2 million per individual ($22.4 million for a married couple)[2] and will be indexed to increase for inflation. As a practical matter, this will remove many individuals from the federal estate tax roll.

Gifts by Children of Appreciated Assets

What strategies emerge from this substantial increase in the lifetime exemption? Many taxpayers whose wealth exceeded the former exemption thresholds made gifts of appreciated stock or real estate to their children in order to stay below those exemption levels. Since the Tax Act did not change the provision that permits a step-up in basis for income tax purposes for assets included in a decedent's estate, the children can now gift these

---

[2] The exemption is $11.18 million per individual and $22.36 million for married couple. To simplify, we have rounded to $11.2 million and $22.4 million.

assets back to their parents, and upon the death of their parents the children can step-up the income tax basis to the fair market value as of the date of death. If the children hold on to the appreciated assets, their basis will be the same as the cost to their parents. Upon sale of these assets, the children will incur income taxes on all of the appreciation in value.

Allocate Assets to the Marital Trust

Another strategy that has become popular due to the Tax Act involves the allocation of assets between the marital trust and the non-marital trust upon the death of the first-to-die of a married couple. Prior to passage of the Tax Act, the usual approach was to allocate the maximum amount of the lifetime exemption to the non-marital trust in order to maximize the wealth that would be exempt from federal estate tax on the second-to-die of the married couple. This still is applicable if a federal estate tax is foreseeable. But this maximum funding of the non-marital trust meant that the basis of these assets would be the value at the death of the first-to-die of the married couple. By increasing the allocation of assets to the marital trust upon the death of the first-to-die, with a corresponding decrease in the amount of assets allocated to the non-marital trust, and by utilizing the increased $22.4 million exemption, the federal estate tax can be avoided and the children can take a stepped-up basis reflecting the value of the marital trust as of the death of the second–to-die.

The Provisions for the Increased Exemption Will "Sunset" in 2025

There are, of course, pitfalls to be avoided. The Tax Act did not make the new exemption permanent. It will "sunset" and terminate at the end of 2025 when the exemption will revert to $5 million per individual plus inflation adjustments since 2011. Clients concerned about the "sunset" might consider making gifts during the intervening period to lock in the exemption. Other clients might take a calculated risk that the federal estate tax exemption never will be rolled back to its prior level, in which case the best strategy is to retain non-cash appreciated assets in order to achieve the step-up in basis that remains an important part of the tax code.

For those who are concerned that the estate tax exemption may be subsequently reduced following the 2025 "sunset," we direct you to the following statistics that we believe indicate that the Goliath, the U.S. government, no longer is interested in collecting revenue upon the death of moderately wealthy taxpayers. In 1998, when the lifetime exemption was $675,000 per individual, the number of estates subject to federal estate tax was approximately 50,000, about 2.25% of the number of adult deaths during that year. By 2013, when the exemption had been raised to $5.25 million per individual, the number of estates subject to federal estate tax shrank to slightly over 5,000, even before the introduction of the increased exemption of $11.2 per individual under the Tax Act. The usual arguments against the federal estate tax – stigmatizing it as a "death tax" requiring a visit to the undertaker and tax collector on the same day, or as a "double tax" duplicating the income tax and therefore amounting to a punishment for working hard and becoming successful – seem to have prevailed. It is likely that in the future the federal estate tax will continue only for the very wealthy in order to avoid creating a large class of "idle rich" and as a driving force to promote charitable gifts by the super-rich.

CHAPTER 1

Move to a Different State

Although the federal estate tax exemption has increased to $22.4 million per couple, Illinois has not changed its $4 million exemption per individual. Also, if a couple is not subject to federal estate tax, the Illinois estate tax, with a maximum rate of 16%, is not deductible against any federal estate tax. The message of the Goliath in this case is clear and unambiguous. If you can, change your residence to one of the many states that do not impose an estate or inheritance tax.[3]

---

[3] Thirty-two states do not have an estate or inheritance tax, including Illinois' neighboring states of Indiana, Michigan, Missouri and Wisconsin, and favored destinations Arizona, California and Florida.

Chapter 2

Reduction of the Corporate Income Tax
Rate for C Corporations

For the years after 2017, the corporate tax rate for C Corporations has been substantially reduced, from 35% to 21%. This reduction is permanent, i.e. there is no "sunset," but of course it is subject to change if Congress and the President decide to do so. Also, the Alternative Minimum Tax ("AMT") for corporations was repealed by the Tax Act.

New tax savings opportunities and strategies have emerged. Consider the following for a wealthy doctor, lawyer, investment advisor, consultant or other taxpayer who has been operating as a partner, proprietor or shareholder of an S Corporation: if no change is made, the taxpayer will pay federal income taxes of approximately 56% on the first $120,000 of taxable income and 40% on the balance.[4] By transferring his or her interest to a C Corporation, the individual's federal income tax will be reduced to 21%. This, of course, assumes that the taxpayer will not require payment of a salary or dividends from the C Corporation, and that the taxpayer will continue the C Corporation until his or her death, at which time the C Corporation can be liquidated tax-free.

This strategy is available to taxpayers who have other funds to finance their ongoing day-to-day living expenses. A taxpayer should consider withdrawing funds from his or her retirement account to finance ongoing living expenses. If the C Corporation technique begins to present any cash flow problems for the owner, it should be possible to elect to become an S Corporation and thereafter withdraw all of the current earnings.

---

[4] The maximum rate under the Tax Act is 37%. To this, we have added 3.8% imposed under the Affordable Care Act and 16% imposed on the first $120,000 as the employer's and employee's share of FICA. The maximum rate to individuals might be greater if the Alternative Minimum Tax is applicable since this continues to apply to individuals even though it was repealed for corporations. This disparity might be reduced if the taxpayer's income qualifies for the 20% Deduction for Business Related Income from Pass-Through Entities.

CHAPTER 2

Every individual, partnership or S Corporation should consider how to trap all or a part of its taxable income into a C Corporation at a 21% rate. The most likely candidates to use a C Corporation are typically doctors, lawyers, investment advisors, consultants and other service providers. But other non-service businesses can employ this strategy as well. This might take the form of a transfer of assets to a C Corporation with a lease back to the transferor, or a transfer of only a portion of a business to a Corporation. Alternatively, you can form a management company that will manage the business, operate as a C Corporation and pay a mere 21% corporate federal income tax on its income.

The taxpayer's arsenal of weapons extends far beyond David's stone and sling. The taxpayer now has nuclear and inter-continental missile capabilities.

Chapter 3

Overcoming the New Limitation for
State and Local Taxes

The Tax Act imposed a $10,000 per year limitation on the amount of the deduction for all state and local taxes. Thus, if the aggregate of all real estate taxes and state income taxes exceeds $10,000 in 2018 or any subsequent year, the excess is not deductible. This will seriously impact taxpayers in states with high income taxes, e.g. California and New York – perhaps not coincidentally states that voted for the Democratic candidate in the 2016 presidential election. While it might be impossible to completely overcome this $10,000 per year limitation, significant benefits can be obtained by diverting income to trusts, even multiple trusts, or to C Corporations that will be eligible to pay and deduct state income taxes, thereby avoiding the limitation imposed by the Tax Act. Another strategy, particularly effective for a decedent's estate or other taxpayer who owns more than one parcel of residential property, is to transfer parcels of residential property to more than one trust so the applicable real estate taxes are not aggregated with other taxes in calculating the $10,000 limitation. If a decedent's estate owns two residences and divides into a marital trust and a non-marital trust, one residence can be transferred to each trust.

Chapter 4

The 20% Deduction for Business Related Income to Owners of Pass-Through Entities

One of the most complicated provisions of the Tax Act, Section 199A of the Internal Revenue Code, provides a Qualified Business Income Deduction (the "QBI Deduction"). This enacts a totally new concept applicable to income from certain Pass-Through entities, e.g., sole proprietorships, single member and multi-member LLCs, partnerships, S Corporations and REITs. For individual taxpayers, the QBI Deduction is a deduction from Adjusted Gross Income and can be claimed in addition to the standard deduction or itemized deductions. The QBI deduction also can be claimed by trusts and estates. However, the QBI Deduction is phased out for owners of professional service businesses and financial service providers whose taxable income exceeds $315,000, and for married couples filing jointly, and is unavailable if the taxable income of the married couple exceeds $415,000. The threshold amounts of taxable income referred to above include all taxable income, i.e. dividends, interest, etc., not merely the income of the Pass-Through entities.

Below is a brief summary of some of the strategies that owners of professional service businesses and financial service providers can use to preserve their entitlement to the QBI Deduction:

- Divert sufficient income to entities such as complex trusts or C Corporations that are not Pass-Through entities to bring your taxable income below the above described threshold amounts.

- Create new Pass-Through entities that are not service businesses and will be eligible for the QBI Deduction without being subject to the limitations if taxable income exceeds the threshold amounts. For example, income earned by a Pass-Through entity formed by a medical practice or a law firm that owns and leases furniture and equipment to a medical practice or law firm should qualify for the QBI Deduction irrespective of the amount of a taxpayer's income.

- A family office or a similar management company that manages the investments of the family should qualify as a business Pass-Through and be entitled to the QBI Deduction. In addition, this management company should be able to deduct investment advisory fees, attorneys' fees and accounting fees that no longer can be claimed as miscellaneous deductions by individuals.

Chapter 5

Other Benefits and Limitations of the Tax Act

Although we do not intend to address all of the various benefits and limitations mandated by the Tax Act, several of these limitations deserve mention:

- In determining gain or loss on the sale of securities that were acquired on different dates or at different prices, the earlier versions of the House and Senate bills eliminated the taxpayer's ability to identify the shares being sold. Under these versions, the shares sold would have been deemed to be the earliest acquired shares ("FIFO" or "first-in, first-out"). The FIFO rule also would have been applicable to gifts to trusts, family members and charities. But at the very last stage of the passage of the Tax Act, this provision repealing the ability to specifically identify securities sold or transferred was removed, and the law remains the same as it was prior to the passage of the Tax Act. Taxpayers are permitted to specifically identify securities sold – the same as has been the case for many years.

- The Tax Act attempted to put an end to the ability to make a tax-free like kind exchange of art. To date, we have not heard of or thought of a plan for addressing this limitation, but there are many talented tax practitioners who represent wealthy collectors of art. Someone will devise a plan.

- The Tax Act increased the amount of the deduction for annual cash gifts to public charities. Under prior law, the deduction was limited to 50% of the taxpayer's Adjusted Gross Income. The Tax Act increased that limit to 60% of Adjusted Gross Income for tax years 2018 to 2025.

- Under the Tax Act, an income tax deduction no longer will be allowed for payments to a college or university if the taxpayer receives the right to purchase tickets for athletic events in a preferred seating area.

- Under prior law, the so-called "Pease rule," named for the representative that introduced this provision, required that all deductions including the charitable deduction be reduced by 3% of the amount by which the taxpayers' Adjusted Gross Income exceeded certain limits, $313,800 for married joint filers and $261,500 for single filers. The Tax Act repealed the "Pease rule" for 2018 through 2025.

Chapter 6

Other Weapons in Taxpayer's Arsenal

Many other tax savings techniques available to the estate planner were mentioned but not elaborated upon in our 2014 book *Avoiding Death Taxes*: grantor retained annuity trusts ("GRATs"); private annuities; self-cancelling installment notes; and qualified personal residence trusts ("QPRTs"). We intend to address these in future publications along with other important estate planning topics: asset protection planning; community property; income taxation of estates and trusts; duties and responsibilities of fiduciaries; trust decanting; problems of non-citizens and estate and gift tax treaties with foreign countries; U.S. taxation of foreign estates, trusts and beneficiaries; operations of private foundations and public charities; probate administration of estates and trusts; and ante-nuptial agreements.

Conclusion

The dramatic confrontation between David and Goliath that occurred about 1020 B.C., when the Israelites faced the Philistines, continues on as a struggle between wealthy taxpayers and governments. The recent Tax Act enacted by the government Goliath introduced new weapons for use by taxpayers.

Numerous battles will be fought between taxpayer David and the government Goliath. Each side will achieve occasional wins and losses. We doubt there will ever be a cessation of hostilities or even a temporary truce. This is an ongoing struggle between patriotic well-intentioned citizens and the governments that they love and seek to uphold. Thus, despite the great pride that we have in our U.S. citizenship and the great affection we have for our country, we predict that this battle with the U.S. government over disposition of wealth will never end. However, the weapons and strategies will continue to change.

CONCLUSION

This book serves as a battle cry to all those faced with the struggle against government-imposed tax laws to preserve their wealth and protect their legacy. Although the government Goliath is large and mighty, it is passive and cannot manage the nimble strategic moves of estate planners who are resourceful and familiar with numerous weapons that can help you meet your objectives. We urge you to seek out and actively participate with an astute estate planning attorney in formulating an estate plan to slay, or significantly weaken, the Goliath you are confronting.